Another Time
Another Age

Jottings from my Godmother

Edited by Delia R. Smith
Foreword by Delia Smith

LENNARD PUBLISHING
a division of Lennard Associates Limited
Mackerye End, Harpenden, Herts AL5 5DR

Published in association with
The Shaftesbury Society

First published in Great Britain 2002
Second impresion 2002

British Library Cataloguing in Publication is available

ISBN 1 85291 148 4

Additional watercolours and cover design by Alison Edgson
Additional calligraphy by Sue Llewelyn Elvidge

Printed and bound in Great Britain
by Butler & Tanner, Frome and London

FOREWORD

As someone who is asked to sign all sorts of things from the back of envelopes to autograph books and souvenir brochures, I am intrigued by this little book. The contributors all seem to have had the appropriate quotation or comforting thought at their fingertips. Did they, I wonder, trot out the same one every time they were asked, or did they painstakingly research some new uplifting message each time?

They certainly never made any spelling mistakes, and often they had a certain artistic talent (both of which I am extremely envious of). But as the title of the book reminds us it was 'another time … another age'. In those days, if you were invited to dinner it wasn't enough to bring a bunch of flowers or a bottle of Rioja. No, you were expected to demonstrate your skill with the piano or the song sheet, or at the very least with pen and ink.

Perhaps it's not surprising that, fortified doubtless by an excellent meal, the contributors to Bertha's book, should for the most part choose inspiring themes such as Hope ('is the sailor on every sea') and Friendship ('the greatest union of minds') and Nobility ('tis only noble to be good'). But it is particularly appropriate that their sentiments should now be gathered together in a collection to benefit a charity where hope, friendship and, yes, nobility are the keynotes.

The Shaftesbury Society has been in business for over 150 years and amongst its ongoing projects is caring for the severely disabled – including the son of the editor of this book (and my namesake!) in the Bournemouth area. Shaftesbury House has to be rebuilt, and this book will help to do it. So buy lots of copies, give them to your friends and remember (to quote a contributor) 'the real joys of life are not the things we get out of it, but those we put into it'.

Delia Smith
April 2002

PROLOGUE

My godmother, whom I always knew as Auntie Buffie, was one of the most remarkable women I have met. I only got to know her late in her life when my husband retired from the Army and we put down some roots an hour or so from her home in Bognor Regis. By then she was a widow in her late 80s. She lived alone, leading an entirely independent life, and I used to visit her every month or so. Her independence of spirit was best indicated when I called upon her once, when she was 94, to find that since my previous visit she had hired a taxi, inspected two possible homes for the elderly, had a 'trial week' in one and had decided to move! We were allowed to help her with that, but by the time of my next visit she had purchased an enormous electric buggy in which she went the three miles to church every Sunday and to the seafront every afternoon – and this having never ridden or driven anything but a bicycle in her youth!

She had a sharpness of mind best indicated by her completion of the main cryptic crossword in the *Daily Telegraph* in little more than half an hour, something which continued daily until a few days before her death aged 98. She also had a wonderfully impish sense of humour, a great interest in others and, above all, a firmly held Christian belief. The latter two qualities were reflected in her will which included legacies to twenty-seven different Christian-based charities, many connected with missionary work overseas.

I like to think that her character shines through the 'jottings' in this book although, of course, they were all contributed by others. Many I imagine, were friends or relatives who may have stayed overnight and, in return, were invited to complete a page in her album. Because of her own faith, I am sure she would have been delighted that they have been put together in aid of The Shaftesbury Society. She would also be very pleased to know that their publication might be of benefit to my own son who has been a happy resident of Shaftesbury House in Bournemouth for 25 years.

The main part of the book contains items written in the albums and where possible these are reproduced in facsimile. However, the penultimate two pages were found loose in the back of one album. They are in my godmother's handwriting and they aptly reflect her sense of humour. I guess they come from a rather more recent age than the rest of the contents.

Finally, I would like to thank Adrian Stephenson of Lennard Publishing, without whose experience, guidance and encouragement we would never have embarked on the project, and Alison Edgson whose design for the cover and small watercolour illustrations have added a real touch of brightness. I am particularly grateful because both gave their time and expertise entirely freely. Many thanks also to Wooden Spoon Society, the charity of British rugby, for very generously covering the printing costs, and also to the sports journalist Mick Dennis, who kindly helped 'open doors' I would never have managed to get through myself. Lastly, a very special thank you to my namesake for her kindness in writing the Foreword. Without her generous commitment to do so when the book was just a germ of an idea we would never have reached the stage we have.

Delia R. Smith

Farnham
June 2002

"'Tis not the love we get,
but that we give,

Which leaves glad
memories through
the coming years."

J.G.H.
1911

A true friend is hard to gain,
    A trifling thing may lose one,
    Be careful how you make one,
    More careful how you use one.

J.S.Speight.
28-1-11

Write your name
upon my page
For tho' we may sever
Friendship is a heritage
That will last for ever.

M. E. L.
Jan. 20ᵗʰ 191

Friendships.

By friendships, I suppose
you mean the greatest
love, and the greatest
usefulness, and the most
open communication, and the
noblest sufferings, and the
most exemplary faithfulness, and the severest
truth, and the heartiest counsel, and the
greatest union of minds, of which brave
men and women are capable.

Your loving friend,
Annie Hancock.

November 4th 1893.

"Friendship"

As moss will rest upon its stone,
And all its freshness gladly loan
God grant each friendship truly lent,
Be ever loving & willingly spent!

As all the flowers in spring agree,
And dance about in mystic glee,
God grant each friendship's happy spring,
May always keep its noble ring.

As night hath blessings of its kind,
And day will lend its light to find,
God grant each woe a blessing prove,
Each joy a web of sweetness wove.

As to each end the friendships blend,
And each in turn their feet must wend
This shades of darkness yet unknown,
God grant his light, may there be known.

A place in thy memory dearest,
Is all that I claim,
To pause & look back when thou hearest,
The sound of my name.
Another may woo thee dearer,
Another may win and wear,
I care not tho' he be dearer,
If I am remembered there.

6/6/17

"Yus mate I told the gov'nar straight 'no soldiering' for me, I ses, too blinking dangerous"

Last night I held a little hand
So dainty and so neat;
I thought my heart would burst with joy
So wildly did it beat.

No other hand into my soul
Could greater solace bring
Than that I held last night, which was
Four aces and a king

Lc/Cpl A. E. Messer.
19 K K K. C
Banbury 1916

Banbury.

All Boys should love their sisters,
But I so good have grown,
That I love other Boys' sisters,
much better than my own!

Ronald Dick
Sergt.
19th (R) Bn. K.R.R.C.
In Training, Banbury.
9th. April. 1916.

Home:-
'Canny Newcastle.

Volunteers' Drill. (For single young gentlemen)

Fall in love with some young & industrious young woman.

Attention pay to her respectfully & faithfully.

Right face in popping the question like a man

Quick march to her parents & ask their consent.

File right with her to the church & go through the service of matrimony.

Halt & reflect seriously upon the duties which you have now assumed & then perform them.

Right about face from the haunts which you have frequented when single & prefer home

Advance arms to your wife when out walking with her & never let her trail behind

Break off staying out late at night & other bad habits if you wish to make your wife & home happy.

With love.

Yours sincerely

H.H.

Liverpool.
XI. 6. 93.

True Nobility

Howe'er it be it seems to me
'Tis only noble to be good
Kind hearts are more than coronets
And simple faith than Norman blood.

· Tennyson ·

We live in deeds, not years, in thoughts, not breaths,
In feelings, not in figures on a dial,
We should count time by heart throbs,
He most lives,
Who thinks most, feels the noblest, acts the best.

· J. H. Bayley ·

Yours very sincerely
C . B . Gilmour

Golbourne
Nov. 15 th. 1894

The rights of women, what are they!
The right to labour and to pray;
The right to succour in distress;
The right, when others curse, to bless
The right to lead the soul to God,
Along the path the Saviour trod.

F.S.
15.4.16

There is no flock however tended
But one dead lamb is there
There is no fire-place how well defended
But has one vacant chair.

O woman in our hours of ease,
Uncertain, coy, and hard to please
When pain and anguish wring the brow
A ministering angel thou.

To thine own self be true,
And it must follow as the night the
day
Thou canst not then be false to anyone

With the best wishes of an 1894
Cestrian for success and prosperity
J. Austin Lloyd

The young moon's golden shell
o'er the hill
Trembles with lustre, and the
trees are still.

August 29th 1895

M. B.

What is Woman?

Woman
is a female animal with
the power of speech
abnormally developed &
entirely surrounded by a
dress that buttons up the back.
She
is the only animal that
has the power to blush, &
the only one that has
any occasion to.

F. W. B.
7/12/15

Their lips were four red roses on a stalk,

Which in their summer beauty kissed each other.

King Richard III

In the Rainstorms of life
We need an Umbrella.
May yours be upheld
By a handsome young fellow.

H. Busby
27/2/16

An Epigram.

That man must lead a happy life
Who is directed by a wife;
Who's free from matrimonial chains
Is sure to suffer for his pains.

Adam could find no solid peace
Till he beheld a woman's face;
When Eve was given for a mate
Adam was in a happy state.

After reading the above, read
every other line, thus, 1st, 3rd, 2nd 4th

Sincerely Yours
Jim Saam

He put his arm around her waist;

The "colour" left her cheek:

And on the shoulder of his coat,

It shewed up —for a week.

J.R.S.

17·1·21.

A, Loving, Wish.

Bright be the future which lieth before
thee
Loving & loved may'st thou go on thy way
God in his mercy watch tenderly oer thee
Guarding thee ever by night and by day.

D. H.
1911.

· BEST · WISHES · FROM ·

· A · CESTRIAN · OF · 1894

· TED · HOWARD ·

Mary had a little watch,

She swallowed this watch,

sad to say,

Now she is taking Beechams

To pass the time away.

W. H. Churchill

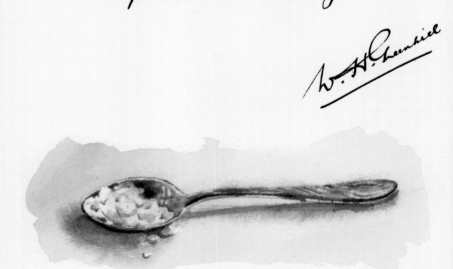

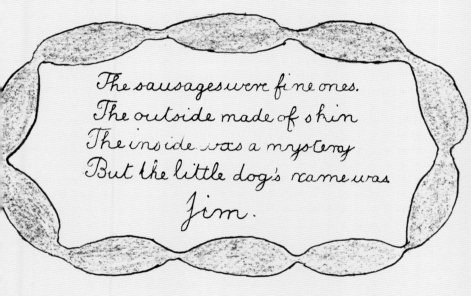

The sausages were fine ones.
The outside made of skin
The inside was a mystery
But the little dog's name was
Jim.

Y.J.
19.1.12.

The real joys of life are not
the the things we get out of it,
but those we put into it.
    There was a time when we
measured our success in life by what
we have, but we now know that
it is how we use what we have
that is true success, as God judges
success.
                Dr. Grenfell.

                        22/5/17

There is nothing half so sweet in Life
As love's young dream:
And next, there's nothing quite so nice
As Strawberries and Cream.

Life is a story, in Volumes Three
The Past, The Present, & yet to be,
The first we've finished & laid away
The second we're reading day by day
The third, & last of volumes three
Is locked from sight God keepeth
the key

Ethel
28.3.17

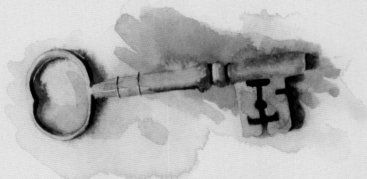

A Thought

So fair God made the world.
    I can but feel,
He surely meant it should
    His love reveal.
All things so work together
    For our good,
Containing truths, but dimly
    Understood.
That what to us seems trouble
    Is but test,
Of faith, that shines but faintly
    In the best.
And could we grasp his purpose
    Spite of fears
We yet should thank Him humbly
    E'en for tears.

June 19. 1910.

M. E. L.

Every morning when you get up, thank
God that you have something to do that
day which must be done, and being
forced to do it, breeds in you a thousand
virtue's the idle never know.

There was a cassowary on the plains
                              of Jimbuctoo
The cassowary ate a missionary
Bible and hymn book too. R.A.M
                                    13.1.21.

जर आम्ही आपलीं पापें पदरीं
घेतों, तर तो विश्वास व
न्यायी आहे म्हणून आमच्या
पापांची क्षमा करील.

JOHN. 1.9.*

James. B. Robinson
Betul. C. P.
India.
June 4th '21

*It would seem that an initial '1' has been missed from the reference because the translation from the Marathi words above is: 'If we acknowledge our sins, then because there is faith and justice, our sins will be forgiven', which is a translation of the first epistle (i.e. 1 John 1.9) rather than the gospel – Ed.

When first we met twas love at sight
  Even before I heard you speak
My heart was thumping with delight
  At once I pressed you to my cheek
Thought I you've beauty, grace & charm
  You'd make my walks a dream of joy
If I could take you on my arm —
  Your company could never cloy

    The question then I had to pop

May Christ, Who gave thee to me as a friend
And in his love unbounded, condescend
To be thy truest & thy dearest friend
    Closer than I could be
That in his bond of love our souls may blend
    In perfect sympathy
And each may daily to his care commend
The threefold being of the absent Friend
    His gift to thee, & me.

God never places a burden upon shoulders unfit to carry it. The work of the world is done by those who are strong, & the suffering is borne by those who are brave. Some times a coward will shift his load & go on, thinking himself free, but he is not. He has lost the power of it himself, & the strength & courage he needed for it, & had at his command to use, have gone divinely, with the burden he laid aside. When you can see the "Why" of things they're no longer hard. The world is perfectly balanced. For every hour of darkness, there is one of daylight, & for every full tide a corresponding ebb, & for every question there is some where an answer.

August 10/1916   Ethel Gorbert.

'BOOKS

'Books, dear books
Have been, and are my comforts day & night.
Adversity, prosperity at home.
Abroad, health, sickness-food or ill report,
The same firm friends, the same refreshments rich,
And source of consolation.

Dr Dodd.

JG April 15th. 1895

Lutterworth Church

When the evening sun is setting
When from care your heart is free
When of others you are thinking
Will you sometimes think of me
    May Gaurdian Angels there soft wings display
And be your guide in every darksome way
In every clime may you most happy be

And when far distant sometimes think
        D. M. H June 1915   of me

Since life is a thorny & difficult path
Where toil is the portion of man
We all should endeavour while passing along
To make it as sweet as we can.

G. H. P.
Castle Ashby

Dont you ~~mind~~ it honey of the
world goes wrong.
    Just be you -
For every cloud I tell you, has
    its silver lines
    Shining bright-
Honey dont you mind the trouble
Life is only just a bubble
    T'will all end right-

Cobh. E.
    May; 5 1916

Put a stout heart to a steep hill,
  Life cannot be a sunlit path
Without one cloud of sorrow.
  But when the sky is overcast,
    Hope for the bright to-morrow.

Annie Enstone.
Nov. 14th 1915.

The Mill.
North Newington.

Hope.

For things can never go badly wrong,
  If the heart be true and the love be strong;
For the mist. if it comes, and the weeping rain,
  Will be changed by love into sunshine again

— / —

Aug 16th 1910.
A.E.R.

There are loyal hearts,
There are spirits brave,
There are souls that are pure & true;
Then give to the world the best you have,
And the best will come back to you.

26/10/10.

MJ

Hope.

Hope is the sailor
   On every sea;
Never a failer
   Or falterer he.
Though the waves rise up,
   Though the skies fall,
Hope ever flies up
   High over all.

—— , ——

16ᵗʰ Aug. 1910.

A.E.K.

" Grumble ? No, whats the good ?
    If it availed, I would,
But it doesn't a bit,
    Not it."

" Laugh ? Yes, why not ?
    'Tis better than crying, a lot,
We were made to be glad
    Not sad."

" Sing ? Why yes, to be sure;
    We shall better endure
If the heart's full of song
    All day long."

——————   Ruth Bulton
                1915.

Build for yourself a strong box.
Fashion each part with care;
When it's as strong as your heart
                can make it,
Put all your troubles there.
Hide in it all thought of your
                failures,
And each bitter cup that you quaff.
Lock all your heartaches within it,
Then sit on the lid and laugh.

F. C. W.

23 · 12 · 16.

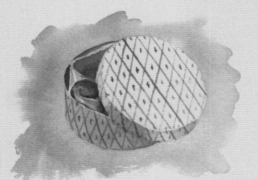

Our Life's Task

We must go on thinking less about
ourselves and more of one another
and so help to make the world a better
place and life a worthier thing—

His Majesty King George VI
in his Empire Broadcast, Christmas 1940.

Surely no nobler task has e'er

Been set by any King

To any People, as the goal

Of life's adventuring:—

To make the world a better place

And life a worthier thing."

Not only has he set the task

He shows the Royal way—

By thinking less about ourselves

In all we do and say,

And more of others, as we live

Our lives from day to day."

Allan Junior.

Three little football fans,
Came from Hull to see
The team they fondly hoped would win
The Match at Coventry.

—

Three little football fans.
Went home so much wiser,
'Twas such a pity, says Coventry City
They hadn't a better Adviser.

—

Three little football fans,
Wisdom now are gaining.
At long long last, their little team
is recovering from their paining.
'Twas a Pity, said Coventry City.
They didn't find time for Training

My godmother was born in Coventry and lived most of her life, until her later years, in that city – Ed.

Beatitudes for friends of the Aged

Blessed are those who understand
    my faltering steps & palsied hand.

Blessed are those who understand my ears today
    must strain to catch the things they say.

Blessed are those who seem to know
    my eyes are dim, my wits are slow.

Blessed are they who looked away
when tea was spilled at tea today.

Blessed are they with cheery smile
    who stop to chat a little while.

Blessed are they who never say
    "You've told that story twice today."

Blessed are they who know the way
To bring back memories of yesterday.

Blessed are they who make it known
    I've lived respected & not alone.

Blessed are those who ease the days
    on my journey Home in many ways.

The old can remember what it was to be
young, but the young cannot know what
                 it is to be old.

I took your album
up to write,
I chose a page
all blank and.
                white.
I dipped my pen
        into the ink.
I knit my brow
and tried to think.
I thought and thought
and thought in vain.
at last I thought
I'd write my name.
        Dorothy Vernon.